The Long Good Bye

Losing Life to Dementia

Kathryn Roberts

DEDICATION

This book is dedicated to caretakers who have stumbled into the world of dementia and struggled to make sense of a disease that makes no sense. It is also dedicated to my Mother, Rose. By the time I knew we should be saying good bye, it was no longer possible. I'd give anything to have those last years again.

ACKNOWLEDGMENTS

I have to say thanks again to my Mother, who had never-ending faith in me as a writer. I'd also like to thank my husband, Elliott, for being patient with me. I'd also like to thank all my team roping friends who were a huge part of the way I coped with the frustration of dealing with dementia. There is nothing better in life than a good husband and good friends.

The Long Good-bye

A guide to some of the things I wish I'd known sooner....

    My Mother raised me, alone, since I was about five and we were a team. Together we took an auto mechanics class, adventured across the country and even built a cabin. She was a very special person who grew up on the South Dakota prairie during the depression and worked her way from secretary to one of the first computer programmers for the Army.

    She was exceptional, not only for what she accomplished, but for whom she was as a person, a woman, a mom, and a friend. She was special. I am no one special, other than I am my Mother's daughter; I have no special connections, I have no special talents, but I found myself facing dementia with my Mother. Our experience was really was an unfolding process, and I was not prepared for anything that followed the initial realization that dementia had struck my family just like it strikes 50% of people over the age of 85. CBS news reported that 35 million people are living with dementia and that it is one of the major causes of disability and dependency among older people.

But, enough with the facts and figures. Millions of them are easy to find on the web. The problem I found with statistics and figures is that they really are a moot point when it happens to you, then the odds are 100%. These are my personal experiences with the lonely, frustrating trip down the back alley of dementia. If I can help one person deal with the frustration and heart-break a little better, then I will be happy. Dementia works slowly at first, then gathers speed, like a roller coaster, and to be fore-warned is to be fore-armed.

My Mother was an opinionated, strong woman, who took care of herself and who lived by herself for over forty years after her divorce from my Father. She was a numbers person. She played the stock market, enjoyed playing cards and took detailed care of her own finances. Probably three years before I even suspected something was wrong, she asked me to oversee her finances, telling me that should she eventually pass away, I would know exactly what was going on. As her only child, I thought that was a very reasonable approach to ageing and I agreed. Not long after, she also started having me drive when I came to see her. She had always been a very independent person, very much in control and these things should have created a small red flag for me. I had always honored and trusted my Mom, and at that moment, I trusted that she was asking these things for me, so that I would be more prepared for the future.

For the next couple of years, I listened to her telling me occasionally things she'd already told me and I told myself that it was just old age coming on and after all, I, myself, occasionally forgot whether or not I had mentioned things to my husband. She became increasingly attached to her kitchen calendar and grew impatient if there was something that had not been entered on it. The calendar, I believe, was one of the ways she attempted to organize parts of her life she privately felt were getting out of control.

All these things, I told myself, were simply due to the fact that she was very detail oriented, very opinionated and...getting old. Looking back, I now realize that I was seeing but did not know or accept that I was already dealing with Mom's early signs of dementia.

At this time, I lived an hour and a half away from her and although I called, my visits were pretty much on a once-a-week basis. At eighty, Mom was a physically active and a busy person with various clubs and activities; a once-a-week visit fit nicely into her schedule as well as mine. When I came down, we often went to lunch at the mall and then walked around to do a little shopping and window snooping. It was our one day a week to yak, plan and just hang out enjoying each other's company.

Over a period of several months, I began to see that she repeated things more often. We had been doing her taxes together for several years now and I could see subtle changes in the meticulous way she kept records. This was a woman who had the paper work for every stock and bond she'd ever bought as well as all the records of their progress for the last forty years, and now she seemed less interested in record-keeping and very much interested in my getting everything done and sent off. Still, I was in denial about something being wrong and chose to think she was just getting old and tired of doing all the details she used to take delight in.

As time went on, Mom started staying home more. There were fewer outings on her calendar and what was there seemed to revolve around doctor's appointments. She said she didn't want to go play cards; she didn't enjoy playing golf anymore, and the luncheons she used to go to with her friends became fewer and fewer and she volunteered less.

She had always been very close-mouthed about her health, but I knew that she never used to go to a doctor unless something was really wrong. I'd ask her and she would give me a fluff answer to satisfy me enough to quiet me, and since my Mother was always the boss and had always been the boss, I was reluctant to push the issue.

In retrospect, maybe I could have been more persistent in the early stages of this process, but that is water under the bridge. As with any health battle, deal with today and pick wisely your skirmishes and where you want to hold your ground. I was not as informed as I could have been on her health conditions because, initially and erroneously, I assumed Mom was still her own boss, making good decisions about her health and dealing well with the management of her own care. Eventually, I found out that she had high cholesterol (hereditary, since I have the same issues) severe osteoporosis, and toward the end, transient mini-strokes.

On my weekly visits, we would sometimes go to lunch with one or more of her friends, and I began to sense some hesitation on their part. The neighbor across the street mentioned often that they were keeping an eye on her. Her friends, who knew only too well what was happening, were as good at keeping her secrets as she was until it began to get out of hand.

Mom continued to get more and more forgetful, although she always knew me and always seemed to know when I was coming. More and more things were lining up and I was beginning to get closer to admitting the fact that there must be something more than old age at work on my Mom. Often now, she couldn't remember names--sometimes, my husband, or her friends. She was increasingly frustrated with some of her own forgetfulness, which she now also openly acknowledged. In conversation, she began to falter; she would forget a word or use one that sounded similar but was different, such as house for horse. I started to wonder what was going on, but at this point, I still couldn't piece it together even though she was already mild to moderately involved with dementia.

As time progressed, sometimes, on my visit day, I could tell she was surprised to see me, and I began to notice a lack of personal care when she dressed or did her hair. It also began to register that she was not taking her pills regularly when before she had been very careful. With her permission, we got a compartmentalized Saturday through Sunday pill container to help her keep track of the days and her medications, but what happened when I filled the box, was that I now saw clearly that her medication routine was haphazard to say the least.

I started at this point to talk with her more specifically about her health and the future. I suggested for the first time that we might look at an assisted living facility, but she was adamant, almost angry, about not leaving her home. My first step across the mother/daughter relationship line had been

7

shot down and was a dismal failure. It was an awkward and uncomfortable moment. I let it rest.

A few weeks later, now more 'tuned in,' I noted Mom's increasing complaints of fatigue (her reason for not golfing) and back and neck pain. Her volunteering information regarding ailments or how she really felt was a new side of Mom with which I was not familiar. This was a pretty clear departure from the stoic, extremely independent person I knew. Thinking back, I realized she had pain problems relating to her osteoporosis well before she expressed them. This made me wonder how long had she been struggling, and how long had she been hiding it (and other things) from me?

One medication she was supposed to be taking was for osteoporosis, and I thought perhaps there was a better one for her since her shoulders were getting more and more rounded. I was frustrated to learn that Mom had decided several years earlier that she wasn't going to take the prescription medication for osteoporosis; she didn't like it and thought it upset her stomach. The multiple spinal compression fractures and stooped-rounded shoulders were the resulting complications associated with that choice. Since her older sister was also stooped, I erroneously thought it was part of getting old and that it was genetic.

The memory loss, fatigue, pain, and other problems like the inability to manage her medicines and personal care suddenly became clear signs to me that there was something wrong. I considered the facts and my conclusion was that Mom was unable take charge of her life (although at this time, I didn't really understand how right-on my discovery was and how much of a change we needed to make). In her own way, I think she knew changes needed to be made, and she wanted to remain independent and make them herself even though she was not able to do so. We were going to have to come to grips with her inability to handle her affairs, something neither of us wanted to admit.

I was forced to start taking more and more charge of her calendar. I started making appointments and taking her to her doctors, since she didn't want to drive anymore and because she told me she wanted a second pair of ears to help remember what the doctor said. I realized she was asking for help in more than one way, but was hesitant to take complete charge.

Time passed. Soon, another year had come and gone and it was time to do her taxes. I paid a little more attention now and I saw that she had a good deal of trouble with simple addition and subtraction or even using a calculator. Her interest in her stocks and other investments was mostly anxiety over the possibility of forgetting to send something in or missing a deadline. No longer could I suspect something was wrong, I now knew something was seriously amiss.

When we went to her doctor, looking for an answer to her multiple problems, Mom sat uncharacteristically quiet in the examination room; I began to try to be discreet and ask different questions regarding the issues I saw and I began to be her peer, and to look at her life in a different way. I saw that she was not the confident, secure woman I'd always known her to be and I knew then that I was now the caregiver. Our roles had effectively changed.

Through some of these new, more private questions I began to ask, I found out that she hadn't been drinking enough water and had suffered through several urinary tract infections (UTI), which can make a person cranky and disoriented. I hoped infection and dehydration was the problem but, when I started dropping hints to her friends regarding her mental health, I found that they too, were worried about her. They told me stories about how she had agreed to go to lunch, then forgotten; they told me how she had gone to have her hair done and not been able to find the shop; she had taken the dog to the groomers, parked the car around the block and then not been able to find the groomers or the car, and more.

At once I realized how blind I had been and how good she had been at hiding the fact that she was having trouble. I didn't know the right questions to ask and I hadn't seen what seemed now, like obvious signs of a problem that had many facets.

I had been calling her in the morning and evening to remind her to take her medications, but didn't realize her friends were doing the same thing, so she might take her pills twice one day and none the next.

I finally talked her into going to see a neurologist--told her it might have something to do with her fatigue--and he confirmed what I now suspected, that my Mother was indeed a victim of moderate dementia. He said she was unable to handle her own affairs, and hearing it from a doctor made it concrete; there was no denying or sugar coating it any longer. I asked what to do and he immediately prescribed a dementia drug as well as a handful of brain and thought-enhancing medications which I was all too ready to purchase and use as directed in the hopes that they would clear up our problem. He avoided saying she was not able to live on her own, and acted as if the drugs would help.

I want to mention here that we had searched for a competent geriatric doctor and found none. I didn't really understand at this point that we needed someone educated and well-versed with the needs of a geriatric patient, because the care approach is very different. At the time I wrote this, there was no medication proven to help dementia either preventative or restorative, and the medications out there are expensive.

Instead, the pill nightmare began. Earlier, she was taking medication for osteoporosis as well as calcium and a complete range of vitamins and minerals suggested by her doctor. The sheer number of pills, dosages, and times they were to be administered had become overwhelming tasks for her to monitor. The swallowing of these pills was also increasingly difficult so it was harder and harder to get her to take them. Consistency was practically non-existent at this point. It became apparent that I was too far away to properly supervise her. Her friends, although they tried, had other things in their life like their own health issues, family obligations and events, and some still had jobs. The long distance was a definite problem in keeping track of Mom; trying to manage things remotely was not feasible.

I began looking at facilities and was horrified at the ones who offered "dementia care" because they all seemed like fancy prisons; small rooms with limited or little or no access to the real world. Frustrated, I put off more investigation of facilities. Looking back I can see they were, in all probability, what her situation called for or would call for in a short while.

I had already looked online to find options and answers,

and found lots of sites that offered assistance or information; all of it was a good start, but I really needed to know more. Quizzing her various doctors was disappointing and their answers were all vague; not one of them suggested she needed to be in a care facility. They had no definitive answers on treatment except to try more medication or a different brand. Understandably, Mom was depressed; who wouldn't be when your world was slowly slipping out of your control? Keep feeding her fish oil, calcium, CoQ10, and all the rest. Which I did--because the doctor said so.

By now, it was very clear, even to the casual observer, that Mom was fully involved with dementia. She would get angry at times because I tried to manage her life. The transition in roles was being forced upon both of us--she was no longer the parent, I was no longer the child and we both were angry, frustrated and wounded by the effects of dementia. Handling this shift of roles was very difficult for me. Mom had raised me alone since I was about five years old and our relationship had always been very clear. She took very good care of me and she was the boss. We were not prepared for the relationship transition nor for her to lose the capability to be boss--or even to be my Mom. Particularly painful were the days she was in a different world. On one occasion she indicated she thought I was her younger sister. Old memories stand up against attack by dementia and in them she found another place and another time; she didn't know she was leaving me behind. I struggled through the next few months trying to reason with her when at this point, she was no longer able to do so and she was very frustrated with my attempts.

Gingerly and reluctantly, I was pushed into a corner and had to approach the question of her moving. She could go to an assisted living facility (something we discussed several times) or she could come live in the apartment my husband and I built at our home for her. Her answer was always a resounding no to both. She didn't want to leave the house she owned and knew and lived in for fifty years and she didn't want to leave her friends. Understandable. She also had a dog, Trapper, that was the center of her life and she wanted to be near the dog. Completely understandable, yet not practical.

Mom had purchased home health care insurance years ago, (again, I think it was when she first suspected things weren't right) but she was now adamant about not having someone come in her home, even though I explained to her that her premiums had already paid for the help. I think she was embarrassed by her growing lack of abilities. She demanded privacy and didn't want meals on wheels, a housekeeper, or anyone to help her with her medication. Living out of town made this impasse difficult for me to manage and I couldn't figure out a way to change her mind. My efforts to persuade her to move or to get her money's worth for needed services continued to be met with refusals.

I was having a hard time trying to make sure she was safe and dealing at the same time with her anger and confusion as I tried to do what I thought was best for her. Things were moving faster now and all things were becoming magnified; medications were a mess no matter what I did, she was still depressed, she didn't want to visit her friends because she was embarrassed by her memory loss and her lack of ability to visit or play cards. Her house-keeping had been falling off for while now and things were scattered all over the cabinets. I had trouble finding important mail (although most of it now came directly to my home address). Her weight was falling off and I knew she wasn't eating healthy, regular meals. She still fought me tooth and nail on moving anywhere or on having anyone come in to help out. I knew she would be so disagreeable if I did something without her consensus, that she would chase away anyone who came in with her anger and bitterness. Again, I felt I had no choice but to be the obedient daughter.

Her friends started calling me when she had trouble navigating familiar places and they tattled pretty regularly now. I was beside myself, trying to get her to move or have someone come in at least part-time and live with her.

Then, one evening, we reached an unexpected turning point. Mom called in a panic and close to hysteria. Someone had broken into her house. She thought they were still there. Now it was my turn to panic. I asked if she had called the police, and she hadn't, so I called them and they came quickly to her house as I sped down the freeway.

When I arrived, the police were still there and said there was no sign of a break in. Mom told them the only thing they stole was her clock radio and she thought they (two girls) were from Sacramento, near where I lived. She then went on to say that I knew them. The officer was very understanding and told me that Mom was disoriented and shouldn't be left alone. I understood perfectly. It was obvious that I had to make a decision without Mom's concurrence and take over management of her life.

There were two sides to that evening. Both of us were scared, however, it provided me with an opportunity to start the ball rolling. I told Mom that she and the dog needed to come home with me that night. I lied and told her it wasn't safe for her since the thieves might come back. Still shaken, she agreed and packed a few things to come stay with me overnight.

That was the last day she spent in her house.

I was so glad to have her home with me and I figured that many of our problems were over now, that she would enjoy living near me and enjoy all the things we could do together. On a full time basis, without an hour and a half travel, I could also oversee her medications, get her to and from doctor appointments, and I could make sure she ate well and got mental stimulation and plenty of rest. But again, that was an erroneous assumption on my part that she soon corrected by sharing her negative feelings about the move and her present predicament on the drive to my house.

Despite her doubts, we settled her in the spare bedroom and for the evening, she seemed fine. I got up the next morning and found her worried and anxious because she didn't know where she was until she saw me. I calmed her, fixed breakfast and then went outside to do my chores (we have a small boarding stable). She didn't remember that I had gone outside and when I returned, I again found her wandering and upset. We live in a rural area on five acres and she had gone out looking for me, but couldn't find me or anyone else, and there was nothing familiar around her. Trapper, her dog, who was deaf and blind, had wandered off and Mom was understandably scared in this foreign environment without her dog companion. Luckily, we found the dog before he reached the creek behind the house.

It took only a few days to find out that I needed to be with her all the time in order to keep her from stressing out and every time she got stressed, she got a little more disoriented. I resigned myself to the fact that now I would take care of my Mother as she had taken care of me for so long. My life had already changed, and would change even more, but it was something I wanted to do and had to do.

To fill the hours and stimulate her mind, I tried to interest her in puzzles, painting or wood carving, all things she'd done and enjoyed before. I found that as long as I was sitting there with her, she would make a small attempt to create something, but if I got up to fix lunch, she stopped and sat quietly, unable to continue on her own.

Mom stayed with me for a week before I realized where we lived was not conducive to her safety. There were rocks, trees, hills, gullies and water--too many places for her to walk off to and too many things that she fretted about and too many places for her dog to wander. When he (the dog) was not where she could see him, she fretted and was anxious about him. No matter how closely I watched them, I was having trouble keeping up with them both. I felt like I couldn't go to the bathroom or take a rest without concern for her safety.

It was time to sit down and have a heart to heart talk with my husband. We discussed the possible options for living arrangements for Mom and the dog. The apartment was not a good solution because she was not where she could see me or where I could monitor her and there were steps that she and the dog couldn't negotiate (something we did not think about when we built the apartment). Having someone come in to help was an option, and that would give me time to clean the barn and feed, unfortunately, I learned the home health care insurance she had purchased didn't cover in home help unless she was in her *own* home or paying rent. Everything was centered upon the fact that she needed to be living in a home of her own to receive any kind of payment for outside help. The insurance company wouldn't budge.

Ok. We can deal with that; basically, we were on our own so I started to deal with the harsh realities of health care and started looking for someone to hire to come in and entertain and take care of her during the day. We would pay the cost out of pocket. I found everything from twenty-four hour live-in help to a part-time nurse, but none of them seemed to be a passable answer. We were not set up for a live-in, nor did we need twenty-four hour care if I was around, the companions I interviewed were not up to dealing with my Mother's stubbornness, and nursing care was more than we needed at that time.

What I found I couldn't deal with was the fact that she was so unhappy in my care. All she wanted was to go back to her home. Since her car was at my house and she could see it, I began to fear that she would get in and try to drive an hour and a half to her house even though she couldn't possibly have found her way home.

While here, Mom began to ask often about her family. She was one of four children and the only survivor. She would ask me how her brother was or how her sisters were doing. I tried to reason with her and tell her that they had passed away and that only sent her into a tizzy. Why hadn't anyone told her they had died? How did they die? There was no way to calm her and once again, I was afraid she would get in her car and try to drive to South Dakota.

After two weeks, my husband and I sat down again and tried to figure out what to do and how to get her into an environment where she could function without so much stress and emotional upheaval. We finally came to the conclusion that I needed to find a safe place for her where she would have supervision. I looked online and found several sites that said they would help find good housing and care for free. I spoke to several and got suggestions from them. I was to go and visit the facilities and decide which was best for my Mother.

In choosing a substitute home, it is important to consider not only the physical and mental condition of the resident, but also personal traits. Having grown up in the depression on the prairie, Mom was a person with simple tastes and all her life, she had known the difference between needs and wants. I knew that anything too fancy would make her uncomfortable and it was important that she be able to keep her dog with her. As are many creative people, she was not an outgoing person, even before the onset of dementia (which would turn out to be an issue later). Online, I found suggestions about the right questions to ask, and they were helpful in a general sort of way. Looking back now, I realize that you not only need to know what questions to ask, but you need to know what answers to expect and what the ideal answers would be. The questions do little good if you have no idea what the right answers are for you. I found that each place wanted you to make an appointment and have a meal there, but the meals and the service were not always the same after you signed up and moved in. There is a reason they want you to make an appointment. Even if they suggest you not drop by unannounced, I would recommend you do it. Busy times are around meals and bed times, and they are reluctant to have you there then because they cannot always have someone to show you around then, but seeing how the staff works during a busy time will give you a clue at whether they have enough caregivers.

I ended up going with an assisted living facility (suggested by an online "helper" who got a kick-back when Mom moved in) that had large apartments so she could bring some of her own furniture. I thought she might settle in better if things around her were more familiar. She could also keep her dog with her. There are more and more assisted living facilities that allow pets now because it is understood that a pet's positive impact makes a significant contribution to the health and attitude of the people in their care.

Her medications would be dispensed regularly and her meals provided in hopes of halting the steady decline of Mom's weight. There would be reminders about going down to eat in the dining hall as well as checks to see how they were doing during the day and night.

As part of the entry process, we had to have a doctor's certification before Mom was accepted at the facility. Of course, the new doctor, in a new city, suggested a whole new group of pills to take. The facility wanted a copy of both, the old doctor's finding and recommendations, as well as the new doctors, and at that point, I was to provide all her medications for them. I should mention here that if she had a headache or needed an over the counter pain pill that, too, had to be prescribed by the doctor. If the caregivers found a bottle of aspirin or antibiotic cream in her room, they would take it from her and I never had any success at getting them back, so I would keep them in my purse. It became important for me to come often enough to give her the over-the-counter pain meds that she needed; the caregivers would give them, but only if the doctor ordered them and then it was not as needed, but all the time whether she needed them or not. At this facility, there was a registered nurse, but no doctor resident, as is the case with most non-medical facilities.

I now had two doctors who certified that she was no longer competent to make her own decisions, and I became her legal guardian and had power of attorney. The roles had officially and legally been reversed. We had reached the point of no return and I had to deal with the fact that I was making arrangements to put my Mother in a home, away from all she knew.

Now what? Well, I had to function and not stall out. We moved Mom in fairly willingly since she was eager to be out of my house, but after a day or so, she realized she was not in her own house and asked when she could go home. That began an unceasing verbal play on her part to leave, of course, as I found with the entertainment attempts, thankfully, she was fairly helpless about actually leaving. Often, she was angry and wanted the keys to her car, and sometimes, she was very sad and depressed. I told myself it was going to work out for the best--Mom seemed to be doing okay physically. She was gaining weight. She walked the dog around the buildings and although she didn't seem to make any friends, she did seem fairly comfortable--not necessarily happy, but comfortable. She was encouraged to sit with the same ladies at meal time and she seemed to enjoy them, although she never wanted to visit or talk with them other than at meal times.

I came to visit almost every day and found her in her room almost every time. In retrospect, that was a warning sign I missed because I didn't know enough about how dementia patients communicate and what their needs were. There was an activity director who had scheduled things for them to do, but the caregivers pretty much left it up to the resident to decide if they wanted to engage in these things. If someone suggested she participate, Mom politely said no and they left it at that. The unseen problem was that she was living in an assisted living facility, but needed more specific medical/dementia care. Whether I was hoping she wasn't as bad as the doctor thought or I just didn't realize the difference between dementia care and an assisted living facility, the fact was, she needed more care than I thought.

Laundry service as well as a weekly room cleaning was provided, but one day when I was throwing her blankets back, I realized that her sheets were not the ones we had provided. Hers was an extra long twin and the sheets on it were too short so the bottoms were loose. When I checked things out, the sheets in her closet were missing pillow cases or were the wrong sets all together. I told the people in charge (the laundry attendants didn't speak enough English for me to communicate with them), but there were several sets of sheets that were never found. We went through this for several months until I got weary of not having the proper things and told them I would do her laundry. It began to eat on me that if they couldn't keep marked laundry straight, then how were other, more important things being handled. My inquiry was answered with 'the caregivers have more training than the laundry staff'.

As I mulled this and a million other things over in my mind, I continued to come every day and eat with her. Then we would normally go take Trapper for a walk around the building. The most common conversation point for her was to either tell me how much she wanted to go home or ask when she was going home. She eventually got around to asking about the location of her car and car keys. Sometimes she would ask the often-repeated questions—how are things were in South Dakota? Or how is my family?" etc. It seemed that she no longer considered me a part of the family she asked about. I no longer told her they were dead. It was pointless.

They are fine.

Everyone is good.

She had a phone and could call me, and did fairly often at first, but most of the time, she didn't remember calling previously. The conversations were normally the same--when do I get to go home and where is my car? I made lists of phone numbers of her friends and my contact numbers and posted them by her telephone; occasionally, when she didn't get confused by the area code, she would call her friends at home.

There were times she called when she was very angry about being there, but wasn't quite sure where "there" was. She had worked in Alaska during WWII and lived in barracks and I think the hallways and multiple rooms made her think she was in the barracks again. She sometimes swore she was in Alaska and about to fly home if she could find her car. She never seemed confused when she thought she was in Alaska or South Dakota; she was very certain where she was then, it was just the time that got away from her. I didn't exist back then, so I was in a kind of limbo with her and I think when she was in a time past, I was more of a moderator for her.

I tried bringing all kinds of things to do. As I said earlier, she used to be very creative, but normally, she would sit and watch me paint or put something together. The best entertainment I found was I Love Lucy CDs, but she could not start or stop the CD player. When I was gone, she sat on her bed and watched TV with her dog. I'm pretty sure most programs made no sense to her, and there were times when something she heard on the news made her worry. I normally tried to leave the TV on a channel that had no news. As another source of distraction, I bought a bird feeder, since she liked to watch the birds, and put it outside her window. Between birds and a couple of pesky squirrels, that provided hours of entertainment.

Then, the worst happened--again. She walked away from the facility and a concerned homeowner called the police who came and picked her up and brought her back. The assisted living manager called me and said there was no way she could stay without moving to the memory care side. No discussion, no options. They moved all her things in an hour and wham bang, she was behind locked doors and it was costing a thousand dollars more per month for the locked doors. I didn't realize that the memory care they provided consisted of only the confinement. I thought the staff would have more and different training than the staff on the assisted living side, but it was a question that never was really asked and certainly not answered in the rush. My Mom was 'in jail' for all intents and purposes and her only crime was dementia. If I had been more aware of the limitations of assisted living/dementia care, I would have had a plan B in place, and would have immediately moved her to a new facility specializing in the care of dementia patients.

It was later determined that she had suffered a small stroke and had been disoriented when she left the facility. After she was moved, she didn't realize she'd moved, but was now in her room more than ever. On our walks, she continued to collect pretty leaves, and we did art projects with leaves and twigs as long as I was there to spearhead the projects and show her what to do. The locked doors didn't change life much except that she could no longer walk the dog outside the building without being accompanied by me or a caregiver. The caregivers were all too busy for that, so it was left up to me.

Now, her phone calls were becoming more numerous during the day and night. She was always angry--sometimes with me and sometimes with the facility. Occasionally she was morose and sad but always the calls were uncomfortable and often ended up with her hanging up on me. She didn't have the ability to dial the numbers for her friends since they needed a different area code and she couldn't make it work, so I was her only outlet.

Even though she was escorted to the dining hall to eat, she often had no interest in food, normally ate like a bird and was now losing weight again and getting weaker. I came and often found that they had allowed her meals to be brought to her in her room, but that she had eaten very little. Housekeeping or a caregiver would remove the full plates and life went on, except for my Mother. She could walk the dog in an enclosed courtyard, but had no interest in that unless I was there to encourage her. She used to like growing flowers and had a great, fragrant and colorful yard in her home, so the facility allowed us to garden in the courtyard, and I planted over a hundred daffodils. Again, she had very little interest in the flowers or the garden.

Due to her increasing muscle weakness, and unstable balance, Mom began to fall. Every unwittnessed fall resulted in the paramedics being called and a subsequent trip to the emergency room. It is part of our legal system to protect the elderly and handicapped from abuse, but in the case of my

Mom, it was only another torture added to her routine. She began to fall often and the trips to emergency were awful for her. By the time the paramedics arrived she probably had forgotten that she had fallen, and when they packed her off to the hospital emergency room, she normally laid on the gurney, waiting for evaluation, until I got there. Strangers were all around her and she didn't know why she was there, or even that she was in a hospital. Most of the time, there was nothing wrong, but as I said before, the unwittnessed fall required a trip to emergency to make sure the facility was not liable or at fault. Fortunately, most of the time, there was no additional injury for Mom, even with the advanced osteoporosis. One word about hospitals, the elderly seem to be treated as if they are already on the way out. We have great hospitals in our area, but I always got the feeling that treating younger patients was a higher priority. You have to be vigilant at every step and fight for the rights of the patient.

I got Mom a walker, thinking it would minimize her falls, but she was not able to use it very much. She was getting weaker and would forget it, especially in her room, where she would fall trying to go to the bathroom. When I got the call, I would rush to her, try to get there before they took her in an ambulance, so I could be with her and take her in the car to save the ambulance charge. Getting her to the hospital was a challenge though. She didn't weight much, but her back was so riddled with fractures that it was getting extremely difficult to move her and she wasn't strong enough to help much.

My husband was very understanding about my sudden departures, the midnight calls from her and everything else, but knew even less than I did about dealing with dementia. Our relationship was being strained by odd hours, missed meals, time alone, and no down time, as well as me dropping everything to go see to Mom. His own parents were deceased and I had already lost my Dad. Mom was my one remaining link to my past and I just couldn't settle for relying on others to look out for her. I know in his head he understood, but it didn't balance the scales. He was suffering from a general lack of companionship. He missed me and I him.

With his support, I recognized that Mom's phone calls, the increasing number of falls, and resulting calls from the facility were not going away or getting better. Without knowing exactly what I was looking for, I set out to find a new place that would accommodate Mom. In a totally frustrated state, I sought out and found a support group, which I should have done a long time ago. There is no need to reinvent the wheel.

I had made my best find yet--a non-profit group that dealt with dementia and caregivers. Information about caring for dementia was broken down into understandable terms. I learned that their reality is not time sensitive. When Mom asked how her parents were, I needed to tell her that they were fine. When she asked where they were, I needed to say they were on the ranch in South Dakota. When she told me she was living in the barracks, I needed to agree.

I also learned that dementia victims should not be given a choice because they will normally say no. It's not "do you want to go eat," it is "let's go eat now". Suddenly I understood why she was never out of her room, and why it was such a problem getting her to agree to a move.

Besides learning how to deal with dementia, I found out there were others who were having many of the same problems, and needed answers just as badly as I did. My frustration level suddenly decreased to a manageable level and I was a better person to live with. I also found out that I, as her legal guardian, had the right to refuse medication for her, even though the doctor prescribed it. Mom had been getting increasingly belligerent about taking her medication since there were a handful of pills including one for osteoporosis, a dementia medicine, an anti-depressant, multi-vitamins, calcium, vitamin D, CoQ10, fish oil, etc. Since part of dementia is increased difficulty swallowing, I was able to get all of these removed except the monthly Boniva and the anti-depressant.

But nothing lasts forever. The falls became more regular, the phone calls ceased, largely because she didn't have the ability to dial the numbers anymore, and she ate less and less. She was wearing diapers and the caregivers took the dog out to walk him, but started complaining that he was having accidents in the apartment. Finally, the management said I had to take her dog home with me. He could visit, but not live with her.

I was worried that Mom would take it hard, but told her that Trapper had to go to the groomer and to the vet and that he would be back later, just like I told her that her car was being serviced and would be back later. She seemed to understand; she loved the dog and I think she knew she wasn't able to care for him any longer. She enjoyed his visits and many times, I left him in her arms while I ran errands. This was one instance when her recollection of time was a blessing; it was enough that Trapper came to visit.

I began to see though, that the accidents on the floor weren't from the dog, they were from Mom not being able to make it to the bathroom soon enough. She had never been able to use the call button effectively. I asked the caregivers about it and they said they would see if she needed to use the bathroom more often. Her accidents from incontinence were also a warning sign that she had inadequate, unknowledgeable supervision and insufficient help. There were plenty of caregivers per patient, but they stayed most of the time in the common area and left Mom in her room because she said she didn't want to go out.

Then I learned that the facility was undergoing management changes as well as an investigation involving their RN misusing drugs for which she was responsible. The news alone was unsettling but then it brought about a push from the facility to standardize all things including medication and supplies like wipes and diapers (ordering from central sources that they picked out). They ordered everything and the bill was sent out to me by the supplier.

It took me several months to straighten out the initial bills and then I found that the facility was using an inordinately large number of supplies. I called the merchant and asked what a normal range was and she agreed I needed to make immediate inquiries. I was once again stressed and frustrated with my inability to set things straight. Then, I also found out that the original doctor's prescriptions (from her home town) were still being ordered, while a whole new set of prescriptions had been ordered by the new local doctor. The old set had never been deleted from her records so she was taking way too many pills. Of course, it was blamed on the RN who was already in trouble. I was frustrated that the facility hadn't seen this obvious problem and my confidence in them was at an all time low. I had considered moving her to a different facility several times before this, but hadn't done so because of the stress it would put on her to move and earlier, because of the dog. But, now I'd had it with this facility. I renewed my search for a new home for Mom.

Then Mom fell and broke her ankle, unwittnessed, of course. All my inquiries about what I thought were improprieties fell on deaf ears and worst of all, she was now in the hospital.

Her stay there was three days total, and of the three, I spent two nights with her, since the first night, she woke up frightened and was inconsolable until I got there. Her oxygen levels were low and she would tear off the oxygen tube if I wasn't there. When a nurse tried to help her or put it back, she would fight and try to bite. She wouldn't eat unless I was there. By this time, she was in the later stages of dementia and there was little I could do for her except be there with her. I felt utterly helpless. The Mom who had cared for and raised me was no longer here and it hurt more than I could ever have known.

Her doctor came in that first day and asked whether or not I wanted palliative care. I had heard only of hospice care where a patient is allowed to go home to die and everyone has agreed to let nature take its course. The only medical actions taken are those to make the patient comfortable. Then he explained palliative care, and it is not as clear cut as Hospice. Basically, I could instruct them to provide only pain medication and prescriptions, and there was a do not resuscitate order (which we already had in place). At that time, he added, she had two weeks to six months to live. At this point, after seeing her frustration and suffering over a period of three years, the news was not the bomb I once thought it would be. Many times I had prayed that she would go to sleep and not wake up to face another day of frustration, fear and uncertainty.

When the hospital discharged her, she was sent to a nursing home, or to what I called living hell. It was fully accredited and was one of those recommended by the hospital patient coordinator, but the home was understaffed and sad. Mom was put in a room with another person, which was OK. The problem lay in the fact that despite how many caregivers were running up and down the halls, no one ever came when the call button was used. Neither person in the room was supposed to go to the bathroom unassisted, and caregivers who had too much to do would come and say they'd be right back, but not show up for an hour. Who can wait that long? Mom had many compression fractures in her back from osteoporosis, and yet the orderlies continued pick her up by the arms and cause her a great deal of pain. She cringed every time they came near her and started complaining about the mean men. It wasn't all their fault though, they were minimum wage earners who had little or no education about dementia or other illnesses. When I came, Mom would be crying and begging me to take her home. I couldn't wait to get her somewhere more suitable and I began again to look.

I had recently heard from the support group that there were facilities that were houses in regular neighborhoods, something quite different than the assisted living or dementia facility. I skipped the internet and went straight to the non-profit group who hosted the support session.

One of the women who worked with them said she knew of several homes and gave me three numbers to call and set up immediate visits at all three. She told me to keep one particular one until last because I would see the difference. She was entirely right. Her mother had been at the third facility and that was the one she personally recommended.

The first two seemed on a par with the facility we'd come from; I was not convinced that the caregivers were anything but paid help who had very little training about dementia. But, the third was indeed different. It was a house that had only six patients and at least two caregivers there all the time. All the patients were seated in the family room which was open to the kitchen where a caregiver was normally preparing the next meal. They specialized in dementia patients, hosted only dementia patients and had a very strict routine since dementia patients felt more comfortable with a routine. There was a reason for everything they did and everything was related to dementia care. I immediately liked the feel of the place and I liked that the patients I saw were clean, relaxed, and would smile at the caregivers when they walked near.

I decided to try it out and the next day I made arrangements to move Mom. It felt right and for the first time, I was fairly certain that this new home for Mom was the right one. I'd learned a lot from my mistakes

It was the best decision I'd made in regards to our dementia experience. I talked with the administrator and owner, at length before making my decision and the things she said were comforting to me. All her employees had been versed in dementia care and they dealt only with dementia victims. She stopped by daily to see how things were going (she had six other care houses) and a registered nurse worked with her and also stopped by daily. I told her about my experiences with the other facilities and she agreed that Mom hadn't been getting the care she needed.

She suggested a doctor that they worked with, as well as a pharmacy. There were no regulations about having to use their contacts, she said only that they had been happy with them in the past. We did switch over because of the fact that there would now be one doctor and one pharmacy and we could resolve a lot of our medication problems.

She explained her mission was to care for her residents so that their family could have a little time off and still be certain things were going to go right. I didn't realize it at the time, but that was the most important thing she said; she and her staff would share the responsibility for my Mom's care. I was stressed out to the maximum with all the hospital and nursing home problems and with the fact that Mom seemed to be declining rapidly. Her goal was for me to take a few days off without worry. I had truly forgotten what a day without worry was.

We moved Mom into her new home; she shared a bedroom with another lady whose dementia was about the same stage as hers and who grew up in Nebraska. Almost immediately, I recognized the fact that Mom was more relaxed and seemed more comfortable (probably because of the homey setting). Her ankle was not healed, so a home health nurse came in to outline a therapy program and show the caregivers how to repeat it daily, which they did perfectly. The routine each morning was for residents to be awakened, then they took turns being showered, and then they ate breakfast together. None of the six residents was allowed to stay in their room unless they were not feeling well. After breakfast, they were seated in the family room where the caregivers often played music, the TV, or did something with them as a group.

Several times I came over (always unannounced) and they were singing or listening to songs. Occasionally, they had entertainment of some kind come in--nothing grand, but it was always special to the residents. It could have been someone who read to them or someone who played the guitar and sang. Over the next few months, I realized that Mom smiled more and seemed to be a little more aware of her surroundings. Occasionally, she would talk a little with her roommate who was seated next to her in the family room. Her decline seemed to have halted substantially.

One of the other things that ended up being a great indication of the level of care she was receiving is that when we moved her in, they suggested we decrease and then cease all together her anti-depressant medication. Their reasoning was that, most of the time, the anti-depressants had a sedative nature and that although it made them easier to deal with, it also made them harder to move around (perhaps being another factor for all the falls). Gradually, we weaned Mom from the anti-depressants, and found that her mood did not change significantly.

As far as her attitude in her new "home", she still asked about her family, she still wanted to go home, and she still got angry that her car was gone--such is the nature of the disease. But physically, she was much more comfortable, had more good and reasonable stimulation when I was not there, and *she never fell again*. If she needed to go to the bathroom, she could call to the caregivers, who were close enough to hear her, and they helped her to the bathroom, which was not the case before and, I believe resulted in most of her falls. They also routinely took their patients to the bathroom.

This facility did not allow the dog to stay with her. At this point, she was not capable of taking care of him and when he was gone, Mom normally did not remember him. They did allow me to bring him in to visit, although it sometimes caused trouble when I took him away or a distraction if she had to do something such as eat. In a short while Trapper developed more physical issues and we had to say good-bye to him, so it was best that he wasn't a big part of her life at the end.

Whenever we had a doctor's appointment, it was routine for the RN or one of the caregivers to go with us so that they were completely informed of what the doctor said, what his orders were, and so they could ask questions if need be. They also ordered medical transport as a routine; I had been struggling to move her by myself when she was weak, and it got even worse when she became wheelchair ridden. No one before suggested something as simple as medical transport, which although it cost a little, was so much easier on Mom since we didn't have to move her out the wheel chair, into the car and then back to the wheel chair.

Mom passed away five months later, from complications of the disease, as most dementia patients do. It weakens every part of a person's body until something gives up.

Her last few months were, I think, the happiest of her dementia journey. Toward the end, there are few things that are really meaningful to dementia victims, and the few eclectic things that remain important are simple. Mom always smiled when I came into the room, and when we talked about her life growing up on the prairie, it always made her feel good. For her, so many things were gone except for a few treasured memories of the good times. Memories that no one and nothing could take from her.

Our good-bye lasted years, and I was the only one who knew we were saying good-bye. I wouldn't have traded a moment with her, I just wish I had known more and above all, I wish dementia hadn't taken her from me so soon.

What I Needed To Know:

The signs of approaching dementia

- Lack of interest in things that used to be important
- Not wanting to visit with friends
- Losing track of time – forgetting appointments or being late
- Getting turned around in familiar places
- Telling things over again
- Anger when questioned about things
- A willingness to be alone
- Lack of housekeeping or the ability to do so
- Lack of ability (willingness) to prepare their own meals
- Lack of ability (willingness) to maintain records
- Lack of ability (willingness) to manage finances
- Wearing the same clothes

The way you feel

- It's only old age – it happens to everyone
- Embarrassment for loved one who seems to be having trouble
- You don't want to admit there may be a problem
- You don't want to deal with a problem

What you really need to do

- Make sure a living will is in order, addressing health care directives and powers of attorney and do it early, when all parties concerned can have input
- Start looking into the possibility of financial aid – veterans benefits, insurance, etc., so that if the time comes suddenly, you won't have

to spend months applying and searching for help

- **Find non-profit support groups** – as soon as you suspect a problem. They can help lead you through the mine field of questions that will develop
- Ask the affected person what they would like--try to involve them in decision-making before they can't make rational decisions
- Start looking at places to live. Even if you think it will not come to that, check out a few places early just in case...
- Be proactive--suspect the worst so you can be better prepared

Dealing with dementia

- There will come a point where you can't do it all
- You will need advice from a support group--one who has no financial interest in your decisions
- Even if you care for your loved one in your home, you will need to find a place with respite care--they offer care for a day, a week-end or a week so you can do other things and maintain a good attitude about caregiving
- Learn to lie. That was very hard for me, but when Mom was asking about her parents and siblings who were already long gone and buried, that was her reality. As far as she knew it was 1945 and telling her she was wrong about the time only threw her into a tail spin. I learned to answer in a way that reassured her instead of upset her. She was where she was at the moment.
- Admit the change of relationship. You are now the parent caring for a child.
- Watch billing, both facility, supplies as well as Medicare, etc. They make mistakes

- Keep a list of the medications given and by which doctor so there aren't overlaps
- Be sure that sedation is not part of the process unless it is really vital
- Try to find a geriatric specialist to go to--other doctors don't really understand age-related diseases or problems.
- Know the difference between palliative care and hospice and be ready to make the decision on both
- If you start out with an assisted living facility, be prepared to move when dementia gets worse if the facility does not have a program tailored for dementia with caregivers who had had training specific to dementia (not just 8 hours, either).
- Reassess with every visit to see if more supervision is needed
- Make complete arrangements for the end. This should be part of the discussion of your loved one when you first suspect dementia. I thought I had everything under control, but when Mom passed away, I had not chosen a funeral home, and had to do so, on the spot, at a time when I didn't need any more stress or need to make any important decisions. Know where the body will be sent, have a casket picked or a cremation plan in order and know where burial or scattering will take place. Make sure you know where the original healthcare directives and powers of attorney are physically located and make sure they are accessible. You will need copies of everything. The end may come more quickly than you think, try to be ready
- Remember that after a certain point, the person you are dealing with is not your mother or father, or sibling. Their mind has changed and their reality is different. When they say unkind things, or are angry, it is not personal, it is an awful symptom of the disease and you should be patient.

- After the point where they are not making rational decisions, don't give them choices, ask them to do something, and ask for one thing at a time. Try to make things simple for them because they need it that way
- Be diligent—don't trust the facility to have the same interest in residents that you do. Most facilities are for--profit and the bottom line is their first concern.
- Have a list of things that indicate a move to a skilled nursing facility or to a place where more medical care can be given. A good doctor will help you make it. Look over the list often and be strong enough to make the move even if there are reasons not to.
- Research and find out state laws pertaining to assisted living, skilled nursing and other dementia facilities.
- Live for each day
- Smile a lot
- Touch a lot--hold hands, give lots of hugs

Some dementia facts

- 6th leading cause of death in us
- 15 million Americans provide unpaid care and payments for care est 200 billion in 2012
- Not normal part of ageing
- Worldwide there are 35.6 million people with dementia and 7.7 new cases per year
- The rate of dementia is projected to double every year
- Dementia has physical, social, and economic impact on caregivers, families and society
- Global societal costs of dementia are estimated to be 604 billion which is 1% of worldwide gross domestic product
- WHO (World Health Organization) recognizes as public health priority

- It is a syndrome – progressive – deterioration of cognitive function affects memory, thinking, orientation, comprehension, calculation, learning capacity, language and judgment , accompanied by deterioration in emotional control, social behavior or motivation.
- Alzheimer's is most common form of dementia
- There is no cure – treatments are in clinical trial stage

Progression of Dementia

- Onset – forgetfulness, losing track of time – lost in familiar places
- Middle – forgetful of recent events and names, lost at home, communication difficulty, need help with personal care, behavior change including wandering and repeated questioning.
- Late – total dependency and inactivity, unaware of time and place, don't recognize relatives, need assisted self care, behavior changes including aggression

Treatment and care of dementia

- Optimize physical health , cognition, activity and well-being with early diagnosis
- Identify and treat accompanying physical illness, detecting and treating behavioral and psychological symptoms.
- Information and long term support of caregivers.

Suggested questions to ask and why you need them answered.

- What is your fall rate? One is too many. They will give you all sorts of facts, such as their percentage according to the average, etc., but be aware that most falls are because of a lack of supervision.

- Ask the ratio of patients to residents. The more mental/medical help the residents need, the higher the number of caregivers needed.
- Ask what else the caregivers are assigned to do besides take care of the residents. If they have a long list of jobs or even one job that requires a lot of attention, then the resident will suffer.
- Ask what training the caregivers have. If it is a short in-house training program, it may not be enough for more advanced cases. The more residents with more advanced dementia, the more training is needed.
- Ask who oversees the medications and who dispenses them as well as who gives them to each resident. In my Mom's case it was almost always someone different who came to her 'pushing pills'. Everything she ever knew told her that it wasn't right to take pills from a stranger. If those who are in charge of medications in any way are rotated, there is a greater chance of error. There should also be some sort of check in place on the person who is responsible for the drugs.
- Ask what language the caretakers speak. I know this is not a politically correct question, but good communication is vital.
- Ask what agencies oversee and what state laws pertain to this facility. This is an important one that you will need to ask of the support group as well as the facilities. Most assisted living facilities are not regulated in most states. Staff to resident numbers, medication procedures, education requirements and standard operating procedures as well as a myriad of other important issues are not defined other than by the facility.
- If you start out in an assisted living facility, ask your doctor to give you a list of things that indicate the need to move to a facility with more medical attention.

- Ask the facility what are the differences between care in the assisted living side versus the memory care side. There should be more training and more supervision; locked doors are not quite so necessary when residents are properly supervised.
- Ask what their fees are, if they will go up, how much they will go up with memory care and if they will go up with Hospice care, so you are better able to plan ahead.
- How many residents are housed in the facility who need complex medical care. The more residents who are non-ambulatory, who have large medication needs, who are non-verbal, who are violent, and who have severe cognitive impairment, the more caregivers are needed.
- What services are available on site. Basic health requirements like housekeeping, laundry, hair styling, and meals are all handled in a myriad of ways and you need to know exactly where they will be eating, how often sheets are changed, how often they are showered (if the resident is not able to do it on their own), how often their room is cleaned, etc..
- Does the facility provide someone to go to doctor's appointments and what kind of transportation is available. When there is an unexpected trip to emergency, will there be someone who goes with the resident to be his or her voice in a strange environment. What is the cost for all these things, if any.
- Will it be documented and shared with the resident's guardian when a resident is not eating. Will a resident be allowed to eat meals in their room.
- Will it also be documented and shared with the resident's guardian when the resident has a sore or a wound.
- Ask to see a year's worth of safety records.
- Check with the Better Business Bureau as well as any other business rating and review establishments in your area.

The end is merciful and the journey is tough. My hope is that with these few words, I can help make the journey make more sense. I can't take away the pain, but I can assure you that others are facing the same decisions and walking the same trail.

May God Bless the weak and reward the ones who care for them......

ABOUT THE AUTHOR

Kathryn is a published romance fiction writer and writes contemporary and historical cowboy heroes that will sweep any woman off her feet. She lives in California with her husband of over forty years. She has been involved with 4-H, California High School Rodeo and they are both competitive team ropers and their newest interest is trialing Border Collie cow dogs.

For more information, go to her web site, kathrynrobertsauthor.com or Kathryn Roberts author on Facebook.

.

Made in the USA
Coppell, TX
02 October 2021

63353054R00030